The UnHeralded Seven Spirits Of GOD

By: Dr. Etienne Graves Jr.

1

Dedication:

I want to dedicate this book to my Father and Mother, Etienne Graves Sr. and Denise Graves and thanked them for always believing in me and for introducing me to the word of God and Jesus Christ at a young age and never giving up on me I love you Dad and Mom this is for you.

I want to dedicate this book to my daughters Janelle and Savannah you are my inspiration in the greatest achievement that I've ever had in this life I thank God for you, and I love you and you are a blessing beyond words.

I would like to also thank and dedicate this manuscript to my sister Shannon Graves. You have always been there for me and I love you with all of my heart. Thank you, Sis, for always supporting and encouraging me. I love you and thank God for you.

Table of Contents

1.
The Unheralded Seven Spirits Of GOD

As I begin to uncover and reveal the true identity of The UnHeralded Seven Spirits Of GOD, I must establish the key connection with the True I.V. and the Lamb slain from the foundation of the world. The correlation between the Seven Spirits Of GOD and the Blood of Jesus is clear and dynamic. Before I delve into the tremendous truth about the "True I.V. of the Lamb of GOD, Let's explore the origin and description of the UnHeralded Seven Spirits Of GOD.

The term, "Seven Spirits of GOD" is only mentioned four times in the scriptures. According to the Bible, the number four represents and is defined as rule, reign, and dominion. "Seven Spirits Of GOD" is only mentioned in the book of Revelations. Ephesians 3:1 states, *"And unto the angel of the church in Sardis write; These things saith that hath the seven Spirits of God and the seven stars; I know thy works, that thou hast a name that thou livest and art dead."*

A Sardis stone is typically and most often a red stone! Why is this important? Well, because the red Blood of The Lamb is the critical reason that we are able to access the Seven Spirits Of God. But the Seven Spirits of God have seven stars.

According to the book of Revelations Chapter One the Seve Stars are the seven Angels. That means that each of the Seven Spirits of God has an Angel assigned to it and accompanies the Seven Spirits of GOD.

4

That number Seven means complete, perfection, and Wholeness. There are Seven spirits of God that have seven angels. Each attribute has an angel and is sent forth with the Seven Spirits of God.

I don't believe in the trinity because the Bible never mentions that, just like the Bible never mentions the word rapture. Do you know where the word trinity comes from? It's a Babylonian term they used in Egypt to express Osiris, Isis and Horus. Osiris as the Father, Isis as the Mother and Horus as the supposed Christ child.

The Bible does say these three bear witness in Heaven, we know this is the Father, Son and the Holy Ghost. It did not mention Jesus, but we know He is the Word. So, people get this in their mind that these three are the trinity. But we don't limit God to a trinity. He is ONE God, we knowthat, but there are manifestations or persons of God; many of them.

Everyone is fixed on the trinity…three, three, three. But think about this. There are seven days in a week. The seventh day is the sabbath. Seven is the number of completion. There is something about this 7. When we look in the Bible and the Lord says "I swear and will not repent," the Bible says "there was no one greater to swear by" so the Lord swore by Himself, talking to the Lord, talking to the Word who was going to be Jesus. He says "thou art a priest forever after the order of Melchizedek".

When the Lord said He swore to Himself, that word swore literally means to seven oneself. I see many manifestations of God, but not just three, not a trinity. I do believe in God; I do believe in Jesus and I do believe in the Holy Spirit and spending time with them individually. I do believe in the Blood and spending time with the Blood and fellowshipping with Him. But I have found at least seven manifestations of God in the Bible. And I am saying at least, there may be many more. Here are some manifestations of God.

1. Father God
2. The Word – which is also the Son and also Jesus
3. The Holy Spirit
4. Melchizedek
5. The Lamb
6. An Eagle – the Word says we shall abide under the feathers of the wings of the Almighty

7. A Lion – the Lion of Judah
8. The Blood – The Blood is separate and has a voice
9. The Anointing (Teaches us)

Could it be the Word, or Jesus, is taking the form of these living creatures? Is it possible the Word is taking the form of Melchizedek or the Word is taking the form of a Lamb or an Eagle, Lion or The Blood? Is the Word taking the form of these?

Or, is there a better or deeper explanation for the Seven Spirits of God? If you are talking about a trinity, how do you explain the 7 spirits of God? You can't. Don't limit God, and don't put Him in a box by what you have been taught traditionally. Let's break tradition and expand your mind so that it will begin to bring revelation that will produce revelation and fruit. That will bring forth change that you will never be the same and that you will catch all these teachings in order to put them together.

Many people say these are the Seven Spirits of God: The Spirit of The Lord, The Spirit of The Fear of the Lord, The Spirit Of Wisdom, The Spirit of Understanding, The Spirit of Counsel, The Spirit of Might. But they are not. It INCLUDES THEM all but these are not the Seven Spirits of God. It's so much greater than just that. It's so much bigger, and much deeper than that.

These by my study, research, and the teaching from the anointing these are the Seven unheralded Spirits of God. The Seven Spirits of God are only mentioned 4 times in the KJV. An Interesting fact, the Seven Spirits of God coincide with the 4 Winds (Nort, South, East, West). That is another topic for Another time. I will show you in another time

Seven represents completion and four represents rule and Dominion. or reign. And the term "Seven Spirits of God" is Only mentioned in the New Testament and only in the book of Revelation. It is one revelation of Jesus Christ.

> *Revelation 1:4*
> *John to the seven churches which are in Asia: Grace be*
> *unto you, and peace, from him which is, and which was, and which is to come; and from the seven Spirits*

6

which are before his throne

This is the first time the Seven Spirits are mentioned and where are they? They are before His throne. These are members of the courts of heaven. The throne is where the courts of Heaven take place. On top of the Blood, on top of our advocate Jesus, the Seven Spirits are also in front of the throne. You have to get through the Seven Spirits of God before you can get to God. They are attendees in the court room of Heaven. What are they connected with? They are connected with the church. I think it is important for us to know about these Seven Spirits because it says seven churches and seven spirits.

Is there a spirit for each church? You bet there is. If there are

seven churches then it's important to know about these seven churches that are before His throne. They are connected to the angel of the church and they're connected to something else.

> *Revelation 3:1*
> *And unto the angel of the church in Sardis write;*
> *These things saith he that hath the seven Spirits of*
> *God, and the seven stars; I know thy works, that thou*
> *hast a name that thou livest, and art dead"*

Now we have added something else to it. Seven stars. What are these seven stars? We let the Bible interpret the Bible. We know the seven spirits relate to the throne, the churches and now connected with the seven stars. What are the seven stars? Let's look in scripture and the Bible will tell us.

> *Revelation 1:20*
> *The mystery of the seven stars which thou sawest in*
> *my right hand, and the seven golden candlesticks. The*
> *seven stars are the angels of the seven churches: and*
> *the seven candlesticks which thou sawest are the*
> *seven churches*

The stars are the seven angels of the churches and the seven candlesticks are the seven churches. What else is associated with the seven spirits of God?

> *Revelation 4:5*
> *And out of the throne proceeded lightnings and*
> *thunderings and voices: and there were seven lamps*

of fire burning before the throne, which are the seven
Spirits of God.

What accompanies these seven spirits of God? Lightnings, thunderings, voices. Not just one but plural. These are connected to the churches, the angels, connected to the throne. Don't you think they are very important? Yes, I do too. They burn like seven lamps. That's why I call them the "unheralded" seven spirits of God. Unheralded means not previously announced or recognized. Who are they really? Not "what have we been taught or told"? What does the Word of God say they are? What does the anointing teach us that they are?

Revelation 5:6
And I beheld, and, lo, in the midst of the throne and of
the four beasts, and in the midst of the elders, stood a
Lamb as it had been slain, having seven horns and
seven eyes, which are the seven spirits of God sent

forth into all the earth.

The four beasts are a Lion, an Ox, an Eagle, a Man with eyes all around him with wings. Elders too. Now we have elders. Catch the Word saying here "sent forth". Like, shoot out, Boom! See this, the seven spirits of God are now connected to the four beasts, the elders, and the Lamb. And the Lamb is wearing them…. the seven Spirits of God. In order to get to the seven Spirits you have to go through the Lamb.

2.
Seven Eyes, Seven Horns Of The Lamb

The Lamb has seven eyes and seven horns. Glory to God. Let's let the Word show us what that means. The word "eyes" there means?

eyes, <u>G3788</u> – ophthalmos – (pronounced of-thal-mos') – the eye, vision, sight, to gaze at with wide open eyes at something remarkable.

The seven eyes, causes you to see. It causes you to have vision, revelation, guidance, discernment, and correction. The seven spirits help you with these instances helping you see things for what it really is. Something being revealed. So, you can have counsel, knowledge, wisdom, understanding and discernment. Not just seven eyes, but also seven horns. What do seven horns represent? Power!

horns - G2768 – (pronounced ker'-as) – to push out, to gore, to shoot out, power

Like when the Word says when the lady touched the hem of Jesus' garment He felt virtue shoot out of Him. It shot out like a horn of power. Electricity, power, fire, heat, whatever, its power.

Exodus 34:29-30

29 And it came to pass, when Moses came down from
mount Sinai with the two tables of testimony in
Moses' hand, when he came down from the
mount, that Moses wist not that the skin of his
face shone while he talked with him. 30 And when
Aaron and all the children of
Israel saw Moses, behold, the skin of his
face shone; and they were afraid to come nigh him
Exodus 34:35
And the children of Israel saw the face of Moses, that
the skin of Moses' face shone: and Moses put the
vail upon his face again, until he went in to
speak with him.

Moses' face was shooting out power of light. There was so much power shooting out of his face they asked him to cover it with a veil. Glory to God. Woooo! The original power of shooting out power comes from the seven spirits of God.

John 4:24
God is a Spirit: and they that
worship him must worship him in spirit and in
truth.

Stop! God is a Spirit. That's what He is. So, if God is a Spirit,
wouldn't it make sense that He would have seven spirits, connected to One. Connected to Him. The Word says those that worship Him MUST worship Him in SPIRIT and in truth. Don't you think we should understand what these spirits are if He is a spirit and we can't even worship Him unless we worship Him in spirit and truth?

Many believe in Isaiah 11 is where the seven Spirits of God are mentioned. But when you see how the Lord gave this revelation, it will bless you and it will help you. This is how the Anointing broke it down and showed me the revelation.

Isaiah 11:1-2
1 And there shall come forth a rod out of the stem of
Jesse, and a Branch shall grow out of his roots: 2 And
the spirit of the LORD shall rest upon him, the spirit of
wisdom and understanding, the spirit of counsel and

might, the spirit of knowledge and of the fear of the
LORD;

This does not say these are the seven Spirits of God. The anointing said "Look at that first verse". Why is He using this terminology? Rod out of a stem?

rod - H2415 - ḥōṭer (pronounced kho'-ter) – a twig or a rod
stem - H1503 - gezaʿ (pronounced geh'-zah) – shoot out
Branch – H5342 - nēṣer (pronounced nay'-tser) – to shoot, to guard, to protect, to maintain, conceal a hidden thing.
Roots – H8328 – *šereš (pronounced sheh'-resh) – the bottom, the deep, the heal of a thing, the root of it, to strike into the soil, pluck away and root out*

So, you have the rod that supports the stem. Then it's talking about a Branch. With a capital B. That means its talking about Jesus, coming to be the Branch. He is The Branch. The issue with this statement that says the root is going to strike into the soil and BOOM! Then it's going to pluck away and root out.

Why is He using this term as a tree? Why is He saying you're going to have a rod (the main branch) and other branches come off the rod. Is it possible this is because they are all connected to one thing? DNA. Roots are DNA, like when we say these are our roots. What grows on the branches? Stems. What grows on the stems? Leaves.

You have one rod, the main branch, that is the Spirit of God. Then you have seven branches, seven rods, that shoot out. Seven stems that shoot out. Seven Spirits, seven stems, all connected to One God. On those stems are what? Leaves. Leaves bear fruit. These seven stems coming off the main branch, which is God, are Spirits of God to help the harvest. The Lamb is the Branch. The rods and leaves shoot out from the Branch.

After the Holy Spirit showed me this, where it's written in the Bible and says He is the Vine and we are the branches planted by the rivers of water that brings forth fruit in a season; it's like we are trees. Like trees of righteousness. It's a likeness to that. Why are these seven Spirits likened to a branch with seven stems shooting out and leaves that shoot out. The stems are the eyes (to see) and the leaves are the horns (the power)

In Isaiah 11:2 you will see Lord is capitalized. The Holy

Spirit was showing me that capitalization was not on accident. It was on purpose to reveal this. "The Spirit of the Lord" is one Spirit. Then, it does not say, "**and** the Spirit of Wisdom". It says, "**The** Spirit of Wisdom". The Spirit of the Lord is one of those branches and the Spirit of Counsel and Might is one of the leaves that comes of the branch called the Spirit of the Lord. Then it says the Spirit **of** the Lord, once again capitalized. Notice the use "of". "Of" being offspring.

There are only two Spirits here. The Spirit of the Lord is #1 and The Fear of the Lord is #2. The Spirit of the Lord has offshoots and connects to counsel and might, and they work together. The Spirit of the Fear of the Lord has wisdom, knowledge and understanding as His offshoot.

1. Spirit of the Lord
   a. Counsel and Might
2. The Spirit of the Fear of the Lord
   a. Wisdom
   b. Knowledge
   c. Understanding

The "commas" used in this verse keeps us connected the two times this is mentioned. There are only two Spirits here. We still have 5 more to be added to. You thought all this time it was just these 7. In Isaiah 11 it speaks of seven Spirits of God that connected to the rod of Jesse but now we can see it's way more than what we originally thought. More than what we had been taught.

Isaiah 11:3
And shall make him of quick understanding in the fear of the LORD: and he shall not judge after the sight of his eyes, neither reprove after the hearing of his ears:

Quick understanding here, has to do with smelling. It has to do with the Spirit of the Fear of the Lord. Very important. So there are only 2 spirits listed here in Isaiah 11. When I say "the Anointing" that's the Spirit of the Lord. He was able to do something. Notice in the scripture below Lord is capitalized.

Judges 3:10
And the Spirit of the LORD came upon him, and he

12

judged Israel, and went out to war: and the LORD delivered Chushanrishathaim king of Mesopotamia into his hand; and his hand prevailed against Chushanrishathaim.

Luke 4:18
The Spirit of the Lord is upon me, because he hath anointed me to preach the gospel to the poor; he hath sent me to heal the brokenhearted, to preach deliverance to the captives, and recovering of sight to the blind, to set at liberty them that are bruised,

The Spirit of the Lord gives you things such as counsel, might and power that you would not have in the natural when the Spirit of the Lord comes upon you.   Because He has sent us to do something.   The Spirit of the Lord anoints you and gives you the ability to do something that you could not otherwise do if He was not upon you.

These are a list of offshoots of the Spirit of the Lord and The Spirit of the Fear of the Lord:

Spirit of the Lord (Isaiah 11:2, Judges 3:10, Luke 4:18)
Counsel and Might

- Spirit of Holiness
- Counsel
- Might
- Power
- Ability

The Spirit of the Fear of the Lord
- Wisdom
- Knowledge
- Understanding
- Treasure
- Revenue
- Prolonged days of life
- Strong confidence

- The ability to depart from evil
- Salvation
- Humility

Proverbs 1:7
The fear of the LORD is the beginning of knowledge:
but fools despise wisdom and instruction.

The Fear of the Lord is connected to knowledge.

Proverbs 9:10
The fear of the LORD is the beginning of wisdom: and
the knowledge of the holy is understanding.

We see right here the Spirit of the Fear of the Lord is the beginning of wisdom, knowledge, and holy understanding. Isn't wisdom, knowledge and mentioned in Isaiah 11? The Fear of the Lord entails, wisdom, knowledge, and holy understanding. If so, how can wisdom, knowledge, and understanding be separate from the Lord of the Seven Spirits of God? According to the Bible in Proverbs 9:10 wisdom, knowledge and holy understanding are offshoots of the Spirit of the Fear of the Lord.

This is why the KJV is so important in teaching. There are treasures, maps, and trails of crumbs that you will see when you study from the KJV, such as, the capitalizations of the word Spirit so, you can find these Spirits identified in the Bible.

The Spirit of Adoption is #3.

Romans 8:15
For ye have not received the spirit of bondage again
to fear; but ye have received the Spirit of adoption,
whereby we cry, Abba, Father.

The Spirit of Grace is #4. Notice the "Son" of God is capitalized.

Hebrews 10:29
Of how much sorer punishment, suppose ye, shall he
be thought worthy, who hath trodden under foot the
Son of God, and hath counted the blood of the
covenant, wherewith he was sanctified, an unholy
thing, and hath done despite unto the Spirit of grace?

The Spirit of Truth is #5.

John 14:17

The woman answered and said, I have no husband.
Jesus said unto her, Thou hast well said, I have no
husband:

The Spirit of <u>Your Father</u> or <u>My Father</u> or <u>Our Father</u> or <u>Revelation</u> is # 6.

Matthew 10:19-20
But when they deliver you up, take no thought how or
what ye shall speak: for it shall be given you in that
same hour what ye shall speak. 20 For it is not ye that
speak, but the Spirit of your Father which speaketh in
you.

The Spirit of Life or The Spirit of the Living God is # 7.

Revelation 11:11 – Spirit of Life
And after three days and an half the Spirit of life from
God entered into them, and they stood upon their feet;
and great fear fell upon them which saw them.
2 Corinthians 3:3 – Spirit of the Living God
Forasmuch as ye are manifestly declared to be the
epistle of Christ ministered by us, written not with ink,
but with the Spirit of the living God; not in tables of
stone, but in fleshy tables of the heart.

An Epistle is something that you write on and Christ writes in us. He writes His name in our heart. And He erases that stuff that's on you like depression, sadness, addiction, divorce and more. He takes away the old corrupt DNA and writes a new DNA on you. He is not writing on us with ink, but in fleshly tables (tablets) of the heart. The Spirit of the Living God can re-write your DNA. He can re-write what has been written in you that has caused you to walk a certain way, look a certain way, act a certain way and so on. But it can be re-written by the Spirit of the Living God.

We have so much more than we thought. How much better are we when we have theses Spirits for us? I did not take away from those traditional seven Spirits. They were expanded. Not individual stems, branches, or leaves, but ALL connected to the root, to the One Branch that is God.

You have to go through Jesus Christ to get to the Seven Spirits of God. You have to go through Him. He says, "I am the

15

way the truth and the life and no one comes to the Father, except through me".

In DNA, the strands are shaped like a ladder and there are rungs in between. These rungs are bases. Adenine, Thymine, Cytosine, Guyenne. Interesting the Spirit of Adoption is "A" like Adenine. The Spirit of Grace is Guyenne. The Spirit of Truth for Theanine. The Spirit of Christ (The Lord) for Cytosine.The actual DNA bases are in these seven Spirits of God. They are connected to us, the seven churches, to the angels, the throne, the courts of heaven, lightnings, thunders, voices it's amazing.

3.
The Spirit Of The Fear Of The Lord

Now, we're talking about the Spirit of the fear of the Lord. So we must understand that term, *"the fear of the Lord,"* is mentioned exactly 30 times in the King James version bible and I use the King James version for many reasons. You can use whatever you want, and it's up to you. I use that and I've explained it many times. Why? Because many different translations have words that they've taken out.

Why is the *fear of the Lord* mentioned 30 times? Maybe because the number three means to conform. He's one God but he can manifest as several different persons and those persons can all come back into one. Three means to conform. So, 30 means acceptably conformed or maturely conformed. The *fear of the Lord* brings maturity and takes you into a mature state. Not just children of God but sons and mature daughters as sons of God. Glory to God.

When the Bible refers to when the fear of the Lord fell on somebody, like when it fell on a nation or on the people what does that mean? It's the Hebrew word *pachad* and it literally means fearful and dreadful, but it brings a sudden alarm out of nowhere. It's a shock; it's like the September 911 attacks that were *pachad* and it was an alarming fear. It was a shock out of nowhere. When the fear of the Lord falls it's an alarming and it causes people to react one way or the other.

17

The *fear of the Lord* is spoken about in Proverbs concerning wisdom is the Hebrew word *yira* and it means to fear morally. An example would be as if I steal this candy bar and I get caught I will be punished for it. It is a reverence of fear. Which means to give respect or honor in an awesome way. Similar to how in certain countries when Kings walk into the room they bow. Reverence in a way similar to when a lady is walking to a door the man should open the door for the lady. Or like when the lady is at the table and she's getting up to excuse herself the man stands in reverence. It's a respect and an acknowledged honor. The Spirit Of The Fear Of The Lord also means dreadfully, exceedingly, afraid. Fearful as Frightened or terrible. Usually when you hear that word terrible you think of terror, but *the fear of the Lord* is the moral reverence, and the moral fear of the Lord. Look at Proverbs Chapter 23:17 and I'm going to advise you to look in your Strong's concordance or look up that term fear of the Lord in the KJV and it will bless you if you read every single one of those instances or inserts where the fear of the Lord is mentioned.

Proverbs 23:17, States, "Let not thine heart envy sinners: but be thou in the fear of the Lord all the day long."

In Isaiah 11 it is widely believed that the Spirit of wisdom is separate without going through the fear of the Lord.
The two go together and they are married. The Lord is married to wisdom with children named knowledge and understanding.
When we talk about the seven colors, the color of the fear of the Lord is the color purple. Because purple represent majesty as in when reference the king you'll give honor to his majesty, to his highness. So, the fear of the Lord is purple spirited fear of the Lord.

The Spirit of the Lord is orange for power and energy. Think about how Bengals and tigers are orange and represent energy. Fire is also represented by the color orange. But the Spirit of the fear of the Lord is purple reverence majesty ground. Proverbs 23:17 says this, "let not thine heart envy sinners but let thine heart envy sinners: but be thou in the fear of the Lord all the day long." So, in this verse he's saying you may see sinners having riches and living their life doing what the Aleister Crowley theme calls for, "*do what thou wilt.*" Do whatever you want to do without being concerned with the consequences.

You may see congressmen, actors, and athletes doing all

kind of wretched morally reprehensive things and you see no consequences because they're sinners and your heart envies them while we wish we could do stuff and get away with it and not have to have any fear of the Lord or not have to have any concern about any consequences, and just live carefree. But then it says, *"be thou in the fear of the Lord all the day long,"* we're supposed to live all of our days in the fear of the Lord. What does that mean for us as believers, because we believe that God is always watching. Remember the seven Spirit's and the seven eyed, seven horned Lamb. He's always watching. The number seven is all over the Bible.

The fear of the Lord is depicted in the story of the Ark Of The Covenant. In 2 Samuel 6:6-10. Uzzah (pride) lacked wisdom and understanding concerning the fear of the Lord and was killed because of it. King David was afraid of the Lord and it resulted in a healthy reverent fear of Him. The Bible said it happened at Perez-Uzzah which means God broke out upon him.

In Exodus 19:16-18 it states, 16. "And it came to pass on the third day in the morning, that there were thunders and lightnings, and a thick cloud upon the mount, and the voice of the trumpet exceeding loud; so that all the people that was un the camp **trembled.** 17. And Moses brought forth the people out of the camp to meet with God; and they stood at the nether part of the mount. 18. and Mount Sinai was altogether on a smoke, because the Lord descended upon it in fire: and the smoke thereof ascended as the smoke of a furnace, and the whole mountain **quaked** greatly."

The word, "trembled," is the Hebrew word *Charad*. It means to shutter with terror, to fear, to hasten with anxiety, be careful, quake, and discomfit. The fear of the Lord brings a shaking. like the Melchizedek anointing, it causes a shaking and a trembling, like the glory of God where no flesh can glory in his presence. Even Paul said in second Corinthians chapter 5 verse 1, "knowing the terror of The Lord."

The word terror is the Greek word *phobos* where we get the English word phobia, and it is defined as to be put in fear, alarm or fright, exceedingly fear. Similar to when men experienced the glory of God or an Angel in the glory of God they fell down as dead. The anointing enables, but the glory disables.

We read in Exodus chapter 33 verses 20-23, 20. "And he said, thou canst not see my face: for there shall no man see me, and live. 21. And the Lord said, behold there is a place by me end thou shalt stand upon a rock and will cover the with my hand while I pass by: 23. And I will take away my hand, and thou shalt see my back parts but my face shall not be seen."

He told Moses no man can see my face and live. His face cannot be seen by humans Who are alive. But in the Book of the Secrets of Enoch, we read in chapter 22 verses one through 5, That Enoch saw the face of the Lord God and he was terrified. Remember Enoch was taken by God to be with Him. So, he did not live. Wow! The anointing of the Spirit of the fear of the Lord brings fear on those who witness his unveiled glory.

When Moses would go to the peak of Mount Sinai, we are told in Hebrews chapter 12 verse 21 that, "so terrible was the site that I exceedingly fear and quake." The word fear there is the Greek word *ekpfobos* - frightened out of one's wits, afraid. This emulates the encounter that I had with Moses, that is referred to in my book, "Dawn of a New E.R.A."

In Exodus 34:29,30,35 it states, 29." And it came to pass, when Moses came down from Mount Sinai with the two tables of testimony in Moses' hand, when he came down from the mount, that Moses wist not that the skin of his face shone while he talked with him. 30. And when Aaron and all the children of Israel saw Moses, behold the skin of his face shown; And they were afraid to come nigh him. 35. And the children of Israel saw the face of Moses, that the skin of Moses' face shone: And Moses put the vail upon his face again, until he went in to speak with him."

His face shone and they were afraid because God spoke like the voice of a trumpet (shofar). They were afraid but then they obeyed. The word shone is the Hebrew word *qaran*- To push or gore, to shoot out horns, have raised, shine, have horns, power, and ray of light. The Spirit of the fear of the Lord is displayed when God shines his unveiled face of his glory. This could change us, our families, cities, neighborhoods, nations, churches, and the world.

What is the final result of the Spirit of the fear of the Lord? It brings wisdom, understanding, and knowledge. The only time in the New Testament the term fear of the Lord is mentioned is in the book of Acts Chapter 9 verse 31. it states, "then had the churches rest throughout all Judea and Galilee and Samaria, and were edified; and walking in the fear of the Lord, and in the comfort of the Holy Ghost, were multiplied."

After Ananias and Sapphira died the fear of the Lord fell on the people. Ananias and Saphira had no wisdom understanding or knowledge about lying to the Holy Ghost. When we don't reverence the Spirit of the fear of the Lord it could result in death as seen by Peter's pronouncement upon them.

The Spirit of the fear of the Lord brings rest to churches. In this passage the word rest is the Greek word *Eirene*- to join, peace, Prosperity(success), kindness. The Spirit of the fear of the Lord brings wisdom, knowledge, and understanding, which will instruct us on what to do, how to do it, when to do it, and where to do it.

The Spirit of the fear of the Lord releases and pours out this anointing. Well, how do we receive this Spirit and receive reference for him in a way that releases us from sin, through prayer repentance,preference, and loyalty? We ask him for wisdom, knowledge, and understanding in all situations and in essence we are asking for the Spirit of the fear of the Lord. It might require us to wait and spend time in prayer and meditation to develop a relationship with the Holy Spirit in order to receive it. Remember in Isaiah Chapter 11 verses three and four he says, "I will make him a quick understanding." In the Greek that means smell by implication, to perceive, to anticipate, to enjoy, except, blow, and touch. It is discernment. Repent now so you can ask the Holy Spirit to smear and rub the anointing of the fear of the Lord upon you and your family, city, neighborhood, and churches for change.

Another result of the Spirit of the fear of the Lord is rest, prosperity, edification, comfort, multiplication, in knowledge, wisdom, and understanding. it brings a closer walk with the Lord God it may even cause you to tremble, quake, and have a reverent fear of the Lord that brings and results in change and the maturing of the true sons and daughters of God. The next Spirit we would talk about will be the Spirit of the Lord.

4.
The Spirit Of The Lord

Before we talk about another one of the seven Spirits of the Lord, it is imperative that I remind you that we must go to and through the lamb which is Jesus Christ to receive the Seven Spirits of God. In Isaiah Chapter 11 verses one through 3 we're told about the Spirit of the Lord and how council and might is the anointing that is released from it. The word anointing means to paint, smear, rub oil, with (ability) council or might.

In Isaiah chapter 40 verse 13 we read, "Who hath directed the Spirit of the Lord, or being his counselor hath taught him?" The word counsel here is the Greek word *etsah* and it is defined as Advice, a plan, advise, deliberate, resolve, and guide. In the book of Judges chapter 3 verse 10 it tells us about this anointing when it states, "And the Spirit of the Lord came upon him, and he judged Israel, and went out to war: and the Lord delivered Chushan-rishathaim king of Mesopotamia into his hand; And his hand prevailed against Chushan-rishathaim."

The word might is the Hebrew word *Gbuwrah*- meaning force, valor, victory, mastery, act of power, strength, warrior, giant, mighty man. a painted-on anointing in Judges' chapter 14 concerning Samson. We are told that might came upon him. In first Samuel chapter 10 verse 6 we're told about another change that happens when the Spirit of the Lord comes upon a man. It reads, "and the Spirit of the Lord will come upon thee, and thou shalt prophecy with them, and shall be **turned into another man.**"

When the Spirit of the Lord is upon you it turns you into another man. The term "horns of oil," is a reference to the representation of the anointing in first Samuel chapter 16 verse 13.

We are told that the Spirit of the Lord provides a standard of protection in Isaiah chapter 59 verse 19, "So shall they fear the name of the Lord from the West, and his glory from the rising of the sun. When the enemy shall come in like a flood, the spirit of the Lord shall lift up a standard against him."

In Isaiah chapter 63 verse 14 we are told that the Spirit of the Lord will cause you to rest. "As a beast go down into the valley, the Spirit of the Lord caused him to rest: so didst thou lead thy people, to make thyself a glorious name." The Spirit of the Lord also enables you to speak and prophesy according to Ezekiel Chapter 11 verse 5. "And the Spirit of the Lord fell upon me, and said unto me Speak; thus, sayeth the Lord; Thus have you said O House of Israel: for I know the things that come into your mind, every one of them."

We often think that is the power of God that is the motivating force and engine behind all power but according to Zechariah chapter 4 verse six this is not the case. It states, "Then he answered and spake unto me, saying This is the word of the Lord unto Zerubbabel, saying, not by might, nor by power, but by my spirit, sayeth the Lord of hosts." The word power here is the Hebrew word *koach* and it means firm, vigor, a force in a good or a bad sense, capacity, means, produce, ability, able, fruit, substance, and wealth. The power and might behind everything that God does is the Spirit of the Lord.

The Spirit of the Lord is the most important one of the seven Spirits of God.

The real power and might is in the Spirit of the Lord. Look at Micah chapter 3 verse eight it reads, "But truly I am full of power by the Spirit of the Lord, and of judgment, and of might, to declare unto Jacob his transgression, and to Israel his sin."

Not only is the power and might the Spirit of the Lord, but liberty and freedom also comes from the Spirit of the Lord. 2 Corinthians 3:15-18 records, "15. But even until this day, when Moses is read, the vail is upon their heart. 16. Nevertheless when it shall turn to the Lord, the vail shall be taken away. 17. Now the Lord is that Spirit: and where the Spirit of the Lord is, there is liberty. 18. But we all, with open face be holding as in a glass the glory of the Lord, are changed into the same image from glory to glory, even as by the spirit of the Lord."

The Spirit of the Lord releases the anointing of liberty. What is liberty? According to this passage the Greek word for liberty is *eleutheria*, meaning freedom (dome of the free), Legitimate or licentious, or moral or ceremonial freedom. The definition continues as unrestrained to go at pleasure, as a citizen, not a slave, exempt from obligation or liability. It is freedom from bondage, fear, phobias, addiction, lack, sickness, sin, and thoughts. The Spirit of the Lord gives us freedom and liberty and allows us to come and go freely. It transforms us and changes us just like the anointing that turns one into another man. A favor follows us and goes before us where policies, rules, laws, regulations are changed and reversed on our behalf because of freedom.

The Spirit of the Lord is the anointing by the anointer making one anointed. Jesus is the anointed (Christ), and we are anointed by the Spirit of the Lord through the Lamb (Anointer). It results in the anointing as we read in Luke chapter 4 verses 18 and 19. "18. The Spirit of the Lord is upon me because he hath anointed me to preach the gospel to the poor: he has sent me to heal the broken hearted, to preach deliverance to the captives, and recovering of sight to the blind, to set at liberty them that are bruised, 19. To preach the acceptable year of the Lord."

The word anointed here means to furnish what is needed, employ, loan, lend, to act towards one in a given manner. The anointing is drawn to and attracted to lack. Whenever something is lacking, something is missing, or something is broken, it removes that lack and replaces it and furnishes what is needed by supplying what is
missing. The Spirit of the Lord would take the lack and replace that!

Jesus quoted what was written in Isaiah chapter 61 verse one. The Spirit of the Lord rubs and smears and paints (anoints) oil, and power where there is lack and need. One of the seven Spirits of the Lord is the spirit of the Lord, but it is the major Spirit from where all Spirits take attributes and proceed from. Remember he says in the end in the book of Acts chapter 2 verse 17, "And it shall come to pass in the last days, say if God, I will pour out of my spirit upon all flesh:

and your sons and your daughters shall prophecy and your young men shall see visions and your old men shall dream dreams:"

Remember according to Revelation 5:6, the Seven Spirits of God must be sent forth. "And I beheld, and, lo, in the midst of the throne and of the four beasts, and in the midst of the elders, stood a Lamb as it had been slain, having seven horns and seven eyes, which are the seven Spirits of God sent forth into all the earth." The words, *"sent forth,"* is the Greek word *apostello,* meaning set apart, to send out properly on a mission, send away, send forth, to set at liberty.

The Spirit of The Lord is the color yellow or gold representing the Anointing oil of the Lord. It qualifies us to be sons and daughters of the Most High God through the next Spirit that I will address; The Spirit of Adoption.

5.

The Spirit Of Adoption

The Spirit of Adoption represents the color red. Each of the Seven Spirits of The Lord connects with a different color of the Rainbow (7 colors). We usually see the color red associated with things like blood, stop signs, red lights, love, and the heart. The word adoption is only mentioned in the New Testament of the King James version of the Bible five times. I know that many people believe the number five means grace, but I believe the number five represents service and works and the opposite of that, the number fifteen, which does means grace.

The word adoption is mentioned in the book of Romans, Galatians, and Ephesians only. But there is much more revelation that is unparalleled to these five times that it is mentioned. The word adoption is the Greek word *huiothesia,* meaning the placing as a son, adoption, figuratively, Christian sonship in respect to God! Also adoption of children, sons, kinship, make, put, ordain, set forth, settle, and sink down. if you break up the word adoption it's *Ad-option.* It does not matter if you were adopted, or given up for adoption for whatever reason. Whether it was because of hurt, pain, rape, drugs, fear, finances, medical reasons or just a plain choice. God made sure, He added another option besides abortion.

We read in Romans 8:14, "For as many as are led by the Spirit of God, they are the sons of God." The word "led," is the Greek word *ago* is defined as to lead, bring, drive, pass time, induce, carry, and be open. Look at the next verse in Romans chapter 8 verse 15 and it states, "For ye have not received the Spirit of bondage again to fear:

but you have received the spirit of adoption, whereby we cry, Abba, Father." The word **bondage** here is the Greek word *douleia*, which is strikingly close to the English word doula. A doula Is a trained companion who is not a healthcare professional and who supports another person through a significant health-related experience, such as childbirth, miscarriage, induced abortion, Or still birth, or non-reproductive experiences such as dying.

The Greek word *douleia* means slavery, to be a slave voluntarily or involuntarily, to bind, be in bonds, bound. The manifested sons of God have a different relationship with the Father than those who are not sons and daughters. *"It is through faith and our relationship as sons and daughters that we have the privilege of asking whatsoever we will. The son who rushes to the Father, demanding, give me, give me, do this, do that, may not receive because his/ her attitude is wrong, selfish, and imposing. The son who honors, adores, loves, obeys, appreciates, thanks, and eulogizes (bless) the Father, may ask what he will and receive freely." ("Dawn Of A New E.R.A," by Dr. Etienne Graves, page 10).*

The word ABBA in ABBA Father means, Father as vocative from the words, to call, and causing to be fruitful and bring forth fruit. We call on the Father and operate in his authority because He is our Father when we receive the Anointing of the Spirit of Adoption. The Spirit of Adoption bears witness and testifies for us.

We are heirs of the Father and joint heirs with the Son, because we are adopted as sons and daughters. The word heirs is the Greek word *klenoromos,* meaning a sharer, inheritor, a patrimony, and acquisition, heritage, portion. by being airs we break the bread with the father via communion and by the blood. It is by the Blood of the Lamb slain from the foundation of the world that we receive redemption, which comes from the Greek word *apolutrosis,* and is defined as ransom paid in full, riddance, deliverance, to loosen with a redemption, price of atonement.

In Galatians chapter 4 verses four through seven it states, 4. "But when the fullness of the time was come, God sent forth his Son, made of a woman, made under the law, 5. to redeem them that were under the law, that we might receive the adoption of sons. 6. And because ye our sons, God had sent forth the Spirit of his Son into your hearts, crying, ABBA, Father. 7. Wherefore thou art no more a servant, but a son: and if a son, then an heir of God through Christ."

We receive all of who our Father is and so do all the devils in hell and on earth. Therefore, there is something called adoption rights and, in many states, the adopted children have as many rights if not more than the biological children do. It's called a reward of inheritance that comes through the promise of an eternal inheritance and we receive it with authority. What has Jesus inherited? We know he inherited a name that's above all names according to Hebrews chapter one verse 4. "Being made so much better than the angels, as he hath by inheritance obtained a more excellent name than they."

That is what the Spirit of adoption will cause us to inherit. It is what he inherited; power and authority in the name of Jesus. In the book of Saint John chapter one verse 12 it states that we have power to become sons of God. Look at this verse. it reads, "But as many as received him, to them gave He power to become the sons of God, even to them that believe on his name:"

The word power here is not the Greek word *dunamis* as it is usually interpreted, it is the Greek word *exousia* which means authority in the sense of ability and privilege, a magistrate, potentate, delegated influence, jurisdiction which means the right to say and to speak for. It also means liberty, the right to make right and make it right. And first John chapter 4 verse 17 it says "…as he is in this world so are we in this world."

There is power in the Anointing of the Spirit of Adoption and there is an authority that comes through the inherited relationship that we have as sons and daughters with the Father. As persons or *persons,* and all seasons, or *see-sons.* Sons that see.

The Bible tells us that there is Life in the Son and not just power, but power and authority, for all of creation, but especially those who are walking in the Spirit of Adoption as manifested sons and daughters of God. It's an authority that no other creature can have except sons and daughters. Why? Because he loves the sons as his own. Adopted or begotten. Adopted children sometimes have a hard time feeling and being loved and realizing that they're loved, and they feel betrayed, abandoned, self-pity, let down, shame, sadness, guilt, rejection and unloved. Why didn't you want me? Why did you give me up?

Thank God you were adopted and not aborted. Because God added an option *(ad-option)* for you to walk in the destiny that you have been predestinated for and full ordained 4 by our Heavenly Father. You have to know your position as a joint heir through the blood as a son adopted or not. Ephesians 1:5,6 records, 5. "Having predestinated us unto the adoption of children by Jesus Christ to himself, according to the good pleasure of his will, 6. To the praise of the glory of his grace, wherein he hath made us accepted in the beloved.

Through the Spirit of Adoption, we are allowed to be loved, and that is critical. The Anointing of the Spirit of Adoption releases unto you and the power to be loved. Matthew Chapter 12 verse 18 states, "Behold my servant, whom I have chosen; my beloved, in whom my soul is well pleased: I will put my spirit upon him, and he shall show judgment to the Gentiles." Then when you turn over to Matthew Chapter three verse 17 we read this, "And lo a voice from heaven, saying, *This is my beloved Son*, in whom I am well pleased."

The word beloved is the Greek word *agapetos*, and I am sure you noticed the word agape which is one of the Greek words for love in the Bible. It means to love dearly, to love, be loved, to be a friend, to kiss as a mark of love and tenderness, to equip with weapons, and to catch fire and burn.

I don't know if you ever noticed this when you read it but let's look at Matthew Chapter 4 verses six and seven. 6." And he saith unto him, If thou be the Son of God, cast thyself down: but it is written, he shall give his angels charge concerning thee: and in their hands they shall bear thee up, lest at any time thou dash thy foot against a stone. 7. Jesus said unto him, it is written again, Thou shalt not tempt the Lord thy God." Why did the devil leave out the word "*beloved*?" It is interesting to note that the devil did not want Jesus to be reminded that he was the *beloved* Son of God not just The Son of God.

The name David means beloved. David was such a mighty warrior for God and walked in victory because he knew he was loved. In order to be loved we have to tell ourselves, I am loved and I will be loved because I am my Beloved's and He is mine. His banner over us is love. Jesus wasn't just The Son of God he was the Beloved Son of God and the devil did not want to remind him of that or want him to remember that. The Spirit of Adoption brings a remembrance to

29

you and I that we are not just sons and daughters of God but Beloved sons and daughters of God.

Satan tries to tell the adopted, "oh your parents didn't love you, that's why you are adopted, or the family that you are adopted to doesn't love you because you are not of their own blood." These are all lies from the father of lies!

When you come through the Blood of the Lamb you are loved and are qualified to receive the Anointing of the Spirit of Adoption. This anointing is attained by spending time in fellowshipping with the Blood and the Holy Spirit in waiting and talking and listening. So, when the Seven Eyes and the Seven Spirits go to and fro in the earth looking to see who is qualified by the marking by The Blood then the Angel that is attached to that Spirit pours out the colorful anointing over The Blood that's on you.

Remember there is an Angel attached to each of the seven Spirits which makes seven angels that are sent forth to anoint you with that particular Spirit in the name of Jesus Christ of Nazareth. It'll manifest in our heart and in power and miracles as it results in fruit and in change by the release of the Spirit of Adoption in our lives. And this is all made completely possible by the next Spirit which we will talk about in the next chapter the Spirit of Grace.

6.

The Spirit Of Grace

The Spirit of Grace is the fourth of the Seven Spirits of the Lord. We've covered the Spirit of the Fear of the Lord, The Spirit of the Lord, and the Spirit of Adoption. Now the Spirit of grace also as do all of them, come from the slain Lamb that has the Seven Eyes and the Seven Horns, is accompanied by Seven Angels and each has one of the Seven colors of the rainbow. The eyes are looking to see who's ready to receive these anointings and the horns are for the anointing oil of each particular Spirit to be poured out by these Seven Angels.

And we must remember we can only receive their anointing through the blood. the eyes of the Lamb are looking for those who are covered with The Blood literally because of the fellowship with The Blood and the Holy Spirit. So, let's go to the Word of God because the Spirit of Grace is actually mentioned two times in the Bible. Once in the Old Testament and once in the New Testament. Zechariah mentions the seven eyes and seven Spirits going *to and fro* ,and the first mention of it is not coincidentally in Zechariah Chapter 12 verse 10.

"And I will pour upon the House of David, and upon the inhabitants of Jerusalem, the *spirit of grace* and of supplications: and they shall look upon me whom they have pierced, and they shall mourn for him, as one morning for his only son, and shall be in bitterness for him, as one that is in bitterness for his firstborn."

The word grace is the Greek word *chen* which means kindness, favor, to bend or stoop in kindness to add inferior, to incline, decline the slanting rays of evening, grow to an end, abide in camps. Grace and supplication go hand and hand in the Word Supplications is the Greek word *tachaknuwn* Which means earnest prayer, intreaty or to ask earnestly for something. Through grace we receive the gratifying in a manner or an act of the divine influence upon the heart and its reflection in the life that results in acceptable benefit as a favor and gift that brings joy and pleasure and makes us well off with Godspeed.

The color of the rainbow that corresponds with the Spirit of grace is indigo. Is it a coincidence that the word blood has five letters and the word grace has five letters. I don't think so! It is of my opinion that the number five represents service and work. We have five fingers on each hand and five toes on each foot for service, and we have five senses for service. When the Lord added fifteen years to Hezekiah's life he showed him grace. Therefore, I believe the number fifteen represents grace.

The Spirit of grace predestinates us for adoption and allows us to receive redemption. Ephesians chapter one verses six and seven state, "6. to the praise of the glory of his grace, wherein he hath made us accepted in the beloved. 7. In whom we have redemption through his blood, the forgiveness of sins, according to the riches of his grace;"

The Bible definition for the word redemption is the Greek word, *apolutosis*, meaning ransom in full, riddance, Christian salvation, deliverance, atonement, something to loosen with, destroy, dissolve, melt off. It also means (burst, tear), joyful emotions. The Spirit of grace provides redemption which allows us to be free and have any hold broken off of us in the name of Jesus. We then become open to receive that richness, which is the Greek word pluotos, and is defined as wealth (as fullness), literally money, possessions, abundance, to feel, (imbue, influence, supply), furnish and accomplish. How? by the Spirit of grace, and through the blood. It was through the blood that Noah found grace because he was perfect in his bloodline. that's what the Spirit of grace does it redeems us and makes our bloodline clean and pure and perfected through the Blood of the lamb.

We find grace through the spirit of grace and the anointing of one of the seven spirits of God that is rubbed and smeared on us through the Blood of Jesus. The word of God tells us that we are saved by grace through faith (Ephesians 2:7,8).

In second Corinthians Chapter 12 verses 7 through nine we

find out more about grace as we read, "7. And last I should be exalted above measure through the abundance of the revelations, there was given to me a thorn in the flesh, the messenger of Satan to buffet me, last I should be exalted above measure. 8. For this thing I besought the Lord thrice, that it might depart from me. 9. And he said unto me my grace is sufficient for thee for my strength is made perfect in weakness. Most gladly therefore will I rather glory in my infirmities, that the power of Christ may rest the upon me."

Looking at the word sufficient it is the Greek word *arkeo* (which has the word ark in it, where Noah who built the ark found grace). It is defined as through the idea of raising a barrier, to ward off, to avail, be content and be enough. Arkaeo comes from the root word, airo, which means, to take up or away, to sail away (weigh anchor), to expiate sin away (sounds like the blood to me), put away and remove. The thorn could have been removed by his grace through his blood but Paul said he would rather Glory in his infirmities, that the power of Christ may rest upon him. So, the Spirit of grace was there to remove it if he would have allowed it to. The Spirit of grace was there and available and the Bible says it was sufficient. the Hebrew word for sufficient is *day(da-hee),* Which meant it was enough, able, and had the ability.

The Lord has been leading me to go around the country and plead the Blood at the, "E.R.A. Of The Blood Conferences,
Because I believe we have stepped into a new era of the outpouring of heaven and the Age of the Blood. It is a new dispensation where we can receive the seven Spirits of God through the Blood of the slain Lamb.

The Greek word for ages is the word *aion,* meaning course, eternal, beginning, beginning of the world, begin without end, space of time, and to find a space or occasion. Grace is a gift of God, and we can receive it because of the sacrifice of the Lamb who was Jesus Christ and the offering of his Blood. This is quoted in Ephesians chapter 2 verses seven and eight stating, "7. That in the ages to come he might shew the exceeding riches of his grace in his kindness toward us through Christ Jesus. 8. For by grace are you saved through faith; and not of yourselves: it is the gift of God:."

We want this Spirit of grace one of the Seven Spirits of The

Lord, that can be poured out on us and hit the target of our hearts with the arrow of the anointing of the Spirit of grace. It is accompanied by one of the seven angels of the seven Spirits, the Angel of the Spirit of grace. But the seven eyes are looking for the blood, red people, and those that receive counsel and fellowship with the blood that the seven horns can pour out upon us, with oil on top of that blood. The blood is meant to wash and cleanse and purge and qualify you to receive this anointing. When this happens you prophetically will receive as a result of this anointing of the Spirit of grace of the seven Spirits through the Lamb and the Blood, favor.

We are told in Psalms Chapter 5 verse 12 that, "12. For thou, Lord, wilt bless the righteous; With favour wilt thou compass him as with a shield." The word favor is the Greek word *ratsone* (which is like the word ransome, meaning, acceptable, accepted, delight, favor, pleasures of own self, voluntary, to be pleased with, to set affection, enjoy, like, observe, pardon, and reconcile self. The word compass is the Hebrew *wordar*- to encircle for (attack or projection), (to crown). Then the word shield is the Hebrew word *tsinnah* and it means a hook as pointed, a large shield, buckler, target.

So, as we put this all together the Spirit of grace will bring us favor that makes us accept it because the Lord has set his affection upon us to pardon us and reconcile us and causes us to be encircled for protection or to attack the enemy with a shield which is like a pointed hook and makes us a target. It protects us from the darts and arrows of devils. Because we are covered by the Blood through fellowship, and pleading the Blood, so the bow of the indigo arrows of the anointing will hit the red target of the Blood that's upon us.

The Angel of that Spirit of grace will pour on us and in our hearts, grace, favor, and protection in Jesus' name. We can now receive this because we know the truth and if we know the truth the truth will make us free. That leads us to the Spirit of truth that we will define, explain and expound upon in the next Chapter.

7.
The Spirit Of Truth

The next one of the Seven Spirits of the Lord is the Spirit of truth. Remember once again we must go through the Blood of the Lamb and wear the Blood to receive the seven Spirits of God and it is no different concerning the Spirit of truth. The term "Spirit of truth" is mentioned four times in the KJV Bible, and three times in the book of John. It is capitalized all three times that it is mentioned in the Bible.

The word truth is mentioned 224 times in the KJV Bible and is not mentioned in the Book of Revelation at all! If you're wondering why, it is because if something is revealed or uncovered you can see the truth while it is being explained to you so there is no need to tell you that it is true because you can see it with opened eyes. Revelation (Uncovering).

Look at John Chapter 14 verse 17 and it reads, "Even the Spirit of truth; Whom the world cannot receive, because it seeth him not, neither know of him: but ye know him; for he dwelleth with you, and shall be in you." The word truth here is the Greek word *alethia,* and is defined as truly, true, as not concealing, to lid, hid, ignorant of, and unaware. The Spirit of truth removes the cover in order to reveal what is real or what is hidden by a lie. In verse 16 he is identified as the "Comforter." In the Greek it is the word *parakletos* which means consoler, advocate, and intercessor.

And we know if there is a Spirit of truth then there is a lying spirit which is mentioned four times in the Bible. In 2 Chronicles 18:20, 21 the lying spirit is identified. "20. Then there came out a spirit, and stood before the Lord, And said, I will entice him. And the Lord said unto him, Wherewith? 21. And he said, I will go out, and be a lying spirit in the mouth of all his prophets. And the Lord said, thou shalt entice him, and thou shalt also prevail go out, and do Even so."

We know the Bible tells us in the book of Numbers that God is not a man that He should lie. Therefore, this lying spirit is the opposite of God who is the Spirit of truth. The word lying here is the Hebrew word *sheqer,* meaning an untruth, a sham, deceit, falsehood, a lie, cheat, be untrue, and deal falsely. Even more so truth usurps fact. It may be a fact that you are sick, and you can feel it in your bones and see it in your body. But the truth is according to the word of God you are healed by his stripes. When it comes to the word of God even facts can be considered lies.

It also connects to the spirit of error, which opposes the Spirit of Truth. We read in first John chapter 4 verse six that, "We are of God: he that knoweth God heareth us; he that is not of God heareth not us. Hereby no we the spirit of truth, and the spirit of error." The word error is the Greek word *plane* and is defined as, fraudulent, delusion, error, and impostor, misleading, and seducing. Where did seduction begin? Of course, it began in the Garden of Eden. Let us look and see how a lying spirit and the spirit of error work and operate against and counter the Spirit of truth. We are either going to believe a lie or the truth and if you believe one or the other you will act on it. When you act on it, that will begin to change your DNA one way or the other.

A lie questions the truth. We can see the first occurrence of this in the book of Genesis chapter 3 verse one stating, "Now the serpent was more subtle than any beast of the field which the Lord God had made. And he said unto the woman, Yea, hath God said, ye shall not eat of every tree of the garden?" The serpent (*Nacash*) questioned the truth opening the door for a lie. The word subtle is the Hebrew word *aruwm,* meaning cunning in a bad sense, or crafty.

The lying spirit or the spirit of error Begins by starting to question what God has said and if he even really said it. Remember that lying spirit is based on deception, and the Bible tells us that Adam was not deceived but he did operate in the spirit of error. It's not in particular a lying word or a word of error but it's a spirit. And remember the Spirit of truth brings

36

mercy, justice, comfort, healing, freedom, power, grace, and favor.

Look at the book of John chapter one verses 14 and 17. "14. And the Word was made flesh, and dwelt among us, and we beheld his glory, the glory as of the only begotten of the Father, full of grace and **truth**. 17. For the law was given by Moses, but grace and **truth** came by Jesus Christ."

But in John chapter 8 verses 44, and 45 we read this about a liar, ".44. Ye are of your father the devil, and the lusts of your father ye will do. He was a murderer from the beginning, and abode not in the truth, because there is no truth in him. When he speaketh a lie, he speaketh of his own: for he is a liar, and the father of it. 45. And because I tell you the truth, you believe me not." The word liar is the Greek word *pseustes*, meaning a falsifier, uttering untruths and deceiving by falsehood.

The Spirit of God is truth, and the Spirit of truth brings perfection. Going back to the word of God in the book of John chapter 8 verses 31 and 32 we read, "31. Then said Jesus to the those Jews which believed on him, if ye continue in my word, then are ye my disciples indeed; 32. and ye shall know the truth, and the truth shall make you free." The word make and free here is the same Greek word *eleuthero*, defined as to liberate, exempt, and make free. This sounds like the Blood to me! Only the Blood can bring perfection and make us free via the Spirit of truth. It's freedom as the opposing lying spirit puts us in bondage. The Spirit of truth confirms that we are not slaves and are able to come and go at will and not be bound by lies.

The truth is in the Blood of the anointing of the Seven Spirits with the Seven eyes and the seven horns. The Spirit of truth establishes attracts and reveals freedom after the cleansing washing and purging of the Blood through relationship, communion and fellowship with the Blood of Jesus.

Is there any wonder that in the word truth you can find the word hurt? Because a lie can bring hurt. but the truth is He took that hurt on the cross and the Blood removes the hurt and heals it and sets us free. The Spirit of truth will enable us to walk in freedom as we are anointed by the Lord God himself.

The anointing of the Spirit of truth is proclaimed in the book of Second Corinthians Chapter 3 verse 17 when we are told, "Now the Lord is that Spirit: and where the Spirit of the Lord is, there is liberty." The word liberty is the Greek word *eleutheria,* and the definition is freedom, to be free and exempt from obligation or liability.

The Spirit of the Lord is truth and the only way to get free and receive liberty it's about the Spirit of the Lord. We must receive this anointing of the Spirit of the truth through the Seven eyes and the Seven horns through the Blood of the Lamb. This is obtained through intimacy with the Blood of Jesus and receiving the Spirit of truth that will cause us to know the truth and make us free. The Spirit of truth will help us identify a lie and separate it from the truth.

Remember what it says in Luke chapter 4 verses 18 and 19, "18. The Spirit of the Lord is upon me because he hath anointed me to preach the gospel to the poor: he hath sent me to heal the broken hearted, to preach deliverance to the captives, and recovery of sight to the blind, to set at liberty them that are bruised, 19. To preach the acceptable year of the Lord."

We must pray and ask the Lord for the Blood to continue to draw us close to him and deliver us and make us candidates for the anointing of the Spirit of truth as we fellowship in close intimacy with the Blood.

8.
The Spirit Of Our Father (Revelation)

The next Spirit in the Seven Spirits of God is the Spirit of our Father also known as the Revealer of secrets. It is the Spirit of the Father or the Spirit of revelation. As you may realize this Spirit is not mentioned in the book of Isaiah Chapter 11 unless you consider understanding the same as revelation. You can receive revelation and not wisdom, knowledge or understanding, but you can't receive wisdom and knowledge and understanding without revelation.

Let us observe Matthew chapter 10 verses 19 and 20 as it states, "19. But when they deliver you up, take no thought how or what ye shall speak: for it shall be given you in that same hour what ye shall speak. 20. for it is not ye that speak, but the **Spirit of your Father** would speak it in you." Wow! It shall be given of you that same hour what to speak from the Spirit of your Father revealed from heaven?

We have to receive and draw near to this Spirit to be close to the Father and his original intention when He created man (Adam). The Lord God has given us the Holy Ghost as the one that we come close to, in order to reveal the heart of the Father.

The Spirit of the Father is the Revealer. He reveals through dreams, visions, supernatural encounters and visitations, revelation, uncovering, or taking off the cover and showing exactly what something is and isn't. The fear of the Lord brings wisdom and instruction on how to act accordingly. But revelation brings clarity and understanding.

In the book of Matthew Chapter 16 verses 16 through 19 we are able to observe the source of true revelation from Heaven. "16. And Simon Peter answered and said, thou art the Christ the son of the living God. 17. And Jesus answered and said unto him, Blessed art thou, Simon Bar-Jonah: for flesh and blood hath not revealed it unto thee, but my Father which is in heaven. 18. And I say also unto thee, That thou art Peter, and upon this rock I will build my church; and the gates of hell shall not prevail against it. 19. And I will give unto thee the keys of the Kingdom of heaven: and whatsoever thou shalt bind on earth shall be bound in heaven: and whatsoever thou shalt loose on earth shall be loosed in heaven."

He said your Father which is the Spirit of our Father, our Heavenly Father revealed it to him. One of the Seven Spirits is the Revealer of secrets who is the father in heaven and from him comes true revelation. In The Greek the word reveal or revealer is the word *apokalupto*, it means to take off the cover, disclose, and uncover.

We are told more about the revealer of secrets in the book of Daniel chapter two verse 47 as it states, "the king answered unto Daniel, and said, Of a truth it is, that your God is a God of God, and a Lord of kings, and a revealer of secrets, seeing thou could list reveal this secret." In the Hebrew, the word Revealer is the word *glah* defined as to bring over, carry away, (bondage), advertise, depart, disclose, discover, plainly publish, and show and tell.

Jesus was always talking about the Father. His Father, which is our Father. He would say things like, "I go to my Father which is in heaven, or I do what I see my Father doing." Which meant it had to be revealed to him from the father. Jesus is the bridge, way, truth, and life to the Father. The key to receive the anointing of the Spirit of our Father which is the Spirit of revelation is intimacy. We must sit at his feet as he reveals secrets to us from Heaven. As we read in the book of Matthew, the key to the authority in binding and losing it's all based on revelation.

Our Heavenly Father even had an appointed time when he would meet with Adam and Eve. He met with them, "in the cool of the day." We read about this in Genesis chapter 3 verse 8 and it records, "and they heard the voice of the Lord God walking in the garden in the cool of the day: and Adam and his wife hid themselves from the presence of the Lord God amongst the trees of the garden." They had a certain time when they met with him to engage in fellowship and receive revelation from our Heavenly Father.

The anointing of the Spirit of the fear of the Lord brings wisdom, knowledge, and understanding. But the Spirit of our Father (Revealer of secrets) brings invaluable and priceless revelation. And wrapped in this revelation is strategy for victory, overcoming and strategic warfare and recipes for success, favor, and abundance. The Spirit of our Father or revelation correlates with the color blue in the rainbow of the Seven Spirits and seven colors of the rainbow. Blue represents revelation.

9.
The Spirit Of The Living God (Life, DNA)

The seventh and final Spirit of the Seven Spirits of God is The Spirit of the Living God- Life/ DNA. We have already covered 1. the Spirit of the Lord,. 2. The Spirit of the fear of the Lord, 3. The Spirit of our Father (Revelation), 4. The Spirit of adoption, 5. The Spirit of grace, 6. The Spirit of truth, and now, 7. The Spirit of the Living God (Life, DNA).

Once again, we read in revelation chapter 5 verse 6, "And I beheld, and, lo, in the midst of the throne and of the four beasts, and in the midst of the elders, stood a Lamb as it had been slain, having seven horns and seven eyes, which are the seven Spirits of God sent forth into all the earth." The seven eyes and the seven horns are the seven Spirits of God and are accompanied by seven angels and the seven colors of the rainbow.

When we turn to Second Corinthians Chapter three verse 2 we read, "Ye are our epistle written in our hearts, known, and read of all men:" This is the only time this phrase, term, and verbiage is mentioned in the Bible. "Known and read (red). The word epistle is the Greek word *epistello* and it means a written message, letter, or to enjoin by writing that causes one to refrain from and avoid (sin?). The word written is the Greek word *egrappho* (where we get the English word, graph) Meaning to engrave, inscribe, to grave, describe, or write (like DNA is written and encoded). Sounds like the word made flesh, doesn't it? Look at verse 3, "Forasmuch as ye are manifestly

42

declared to be the epistle of Christ ministered by us, written not with ink, but with the Spirit of the living God: not in tables of stone, but in fleshly tables of the heart."

Fleshly tables is the Greek word *plax* and it is defined as a moulding board, a flat surface, to mode, shape and to fabricate form (like DNA). Jesus was the Word made flesh so that we can be flesh that becomes the word, and that is only done by his changing and affecting and regenerating our DNA through the life of the living God. That is why the color that correlates to the Spirit of the living God is connected to the color red for blood. Could this be why in the King James version of the Bible when Jesus speaks it is written in the color red?

The reference to fleshly tables causes us to we recall in the Bible where it says our flesh is as grass and grass is the color green which represents fruitfulness, life, multiplication, growth, reproduction, and regeneration. Think of the trees, plants, grass and bushes all representing the color green. If you're wondering why I mentioned the color green it is because in the Bible it says there was an emerald rainbow around the throne. Look at the book of Revelation Chapter 4 verse 3, "And he that sat was to look up on like a Jasper and a sardine stone: and there was a rainbow round about the throne, in sight like until an emerald." Emeralds are the color green! The negative meaning of the color green is jealousy, envy, and rage. Are you familiar with the term *"green with envy?"* Think about how the enemies of God worshipped idols that couldn't talk or move and were not alive, like Dagon, as for example, green with envy.

The word living in "living God," is the Greek word *zao* (like the English word zoo), which means live, life, quick, to live. In the Greek the word living is the Hebrew word *chay* and is defined as alive, raw, fresh, plant, water, year, life or living thing, age, alive, beast, company, raw, running, spring, troop and to revive, give promise of life, nourish, preserve, quicken, recover, repair, restore, and revive. Maybe now you can recognize where they get Christmas colors of red and green. The anointing of the Spirit of the living God is able to cause our DNA to be revived and recover and be repaired and bring promise of life to quicken us and restore us and nourish us.

Look at First Kings chapter 17 verse 17 and it states, "and it came to pass after these things, that the son of the woman, the mistress of

43

the house, fell sick; and his sickness was so sore, that there was no breath left in him." He was revived and brought back to life by the Spirit of the living God. Then in Mark chapter 5 verse 41and 42, we read this, "41. And he (Jesus) took the damsel by the hand, and said unto her, Talitha cumi; Which is, being interpreted, Damsel so I say unto thee arise. 42. And straightway the damsel arose and walked; But she was of the age of 12 years. And they were astonished with a great astonishment (displacement of mind, bewilderment, amazed, out of wits)." She was revived back to life by the Spirit of the living God!

In Acts 20:9. 10, it states, "9. And there sat in a window a certain man named Eutychus, being fallen into a deep sleep: and as Paul was long preaching, he sunk down with sleep, and fell down from the third loft, and was taken up dead. 10. And Paul went down, and fell on him, embracing him said, Trouble not yourselves; for his life is in him." The Sprit of the living God restored and revived him because the Spirit of the living God brings life and regenerates DNA.

How about the instance when the Spirit of the living God interrupted a funeral procession? Observe Luke 7:11-17, "11. And it came to pass the day after, that he went into a city called Nain; and many of his disciples went with him, and much people. 12. Now when he came nigh to the gate of the city, behold there was a dead man carried out, the only son of his mother, and she was a widow: and much people of the city was with her. 13. And when the Lord saw her, he had compassion on her, and said unto her, weep not. 14. And he came and touched the bier: and they that bear him stood still. And he said, young man, I say unto thee, arise. 15. And he that was dead set up and began to speak. And he delivered him to his mother. 16. and there came a fear on all: and they glorified God, saying, that a great prophet is risen up among us; And, that God had visited his people. 17. And this rumor of him went forth throughout all Judea, and throughout all the region round about."

Only the Spirit of the living God can bring life where there was death. The word Nain means, habitation, house, pasture, green. The anointing of the Spirit of the living God is not just rubbed or smeared on but in us to affect our DNA. The anointing of the oil goes over the blood. So therefore, the anointing, rubbing, and smearing of the living God over the Blood of the slain Lamb will flow out. The Blood has a voice and a frequency that will go out without having to even come into physical contact with the body with the Blood of in the anointing of the Spirit of the living God produces the Spirit of life via the Blood. Life is in the Blood.

Another peculiar coincidence is the terms" living God," and the Word, "Lazarus," It's mentioned exactly 15 times in the Bible. the number 15 represents grace. The Blood speaks and it speaks by the Spirit of the living God which is life. John Chapter 11 verses 41 through 44 states, "41. then they took away the stone from the place where the dead was laid. And Jesus lifted up his eyes, and said, Father, I thank thee that thou hast heard me. 42. And I knew that thou hearest me always: but because of the people which stand by I said it, that they may believe that thou hast sent me. 43. And when he thus had spoken, he cried with a loud voice, Lazarus, come forth. 44. And he that was dead came forth, bound hand and foot with grave clothes: and his face was bound about with the napkin. Jesus saith unto him, Loose him and let him go." Where there is something that is dead the Spirit of the living God brings life to it because of the Blood.

The Spirit of the living God is the Spirit of life. This is confirmed in the book of Romans chapter 8 verses one and two, "1. There is therefore, now no condemnation to them which are in Christ Jesus, who walk not after the flesh, but after the Spirit. 2. For the law of the Spirit of life in Christ Jesus hath made me free from the law of sin and death." The word condemnation is the Greek word *katakrima,* meaning, an adverse sentence, a verdict, to judge against, damn, condemn, sue at law, decide against, and punish. It is the Blood that's sets us free from condemnation and the verdict against us in the courts or the Throne of Heaven. The pleading and applying of the Blood keeps us from condemnation and the judgment against us.

The anointing of the spirit of the living God has an offshoot of regeneration, life, living life, revival, repairing, growth, fruitfulness, resurrection, multiplication, increase, and recreation, in our DNA and Blood.

The Spirit of the Lord is the color orange which represents power. The Spirit of the fear of the Lord is the Color purple which represents his presence. The Spirit of the Father is the color blue which represents revelation. Spirit of adoption is the color red which is the color of blood and represents the bloodline. The Spirit of grace is indigo which represents favor. The Spirit of truth is the color yellow which represents the gift of truth. In the Spirit of the living God is the color green which represents life and life more abundantly.

Seven Spirits and seven colors of the rainbow, and seven anointings and 7 angels. Seven eyes looking for candidates who are wearing the Blood of Jesus and seven horns to pour out the anointing oil of each of these seven Spirits. The slain Lamb past the seven eyes and the seven horns. Worthy is the lamb that was slain to receive power, riches, wisdom, strength, honor, glory, and blessing. There are seven things the Lamb received to correspond with the seven Spirits of God the seven eyes the seven horns the seven colors of the rainbow and the seven angels.

10.

7 Spirits, The Rainbow, And The Blood

In 2015 I was given a vision of a being with a crown and he had a long train of his garment that was following him and it had the colors of the rainbow on it. At first, I thought it was one of the 24 elders because of the 24 hues of the color wheel. But I have come to learn by the Anointing that it was a spiritual being one of the seven spirits or the seven Spirits in one.

The rainbow is a representation of power, energy, force, harmony, and His show of light. The seven colors of the rainbow correspond with the seven Spirits of God and those seven colors are red, orange, yellow, green, blue, indigo, and Violet. The LGBTQ rainbow flag has only six colors and it is missing the color indigo which represents the Spirit of grace. In-digo, where the Latin word digo means to speak or say.

The Spirit of grace brings faith, healing, mercy, love, salvation, sound mind, strength, and meekness. Grace is unmerited favor mercy and kindness. The opposite of the Spirit of grace is disgrace, awkwardness, and deformity. This is where gay pride comes in. The Bible says where sin does abound grace does abound much more. God's rainbow or his bow means much more than we thought. Each color corresponds and parallels to the seven Spirits of God. The word rainbow is mentioned two times in the book of Revelation, and the word bow is mentioned four times in the Old Testament equaling 6 times which is interesting when you think of the six colors of the LGBTQ rainbow.

Have you ever noticed that the rainbow looks like a bow from a bow and arrow? These seven Spirits and seven colors which represent seven anointings are aimed to be *sent forth* into all the earth according to Revelation chapter 5 verse six. Seven Spirits with seven angels sent forth like a bow with an arrow. As if God is shooting out arrows of anointing from the bow and the seven Spirits. This sounds like what was spoken of in Lamentations chapter 3 verse 12, "He hath bent his bow and set me as a mark for the arrow." It seems as though the anointing can be shot forth like arrows for those who are marked for it. That's why there are seven eyes of the seven Spirits looking for those who are qualified candidates wearing and covered by the blood of Jesus.

The rainbow was also like an arc, which is a homophone for ark. think of Noah's ark and the rainbow was given as a sign of a covenant after the flood that the Lord sent to judge the Nephilim. and the covenant stated that he would not flood the earth anymore with water. How Preposterous is it that the LGBTQ community uses this rainbow as a symbol of pride?

The Greek word for rainbow is the word iris meaning, symbol of the female messenger of the Pagan deities. It is from the root word *ereo* meaning to utter, speak, and say. Iris is goddess of the rainbow or messenger of the gods, and the fraternal twin of the god arch. Iris is also, Siri spelled backwards. And iris is also the pupil or center of the eye. The rainbow is similar to the ark of the eye and for those of the New Age, who believe in the all-seeing eye as the source of knowledge and enlightenment. The seven eyes of the seven Spirits are looking to send forth and shoot out horns and arrows of the anointing oil of these Spirits.

Let's look at Genesis Chapter 9 verses 11 through 17, "11. And I will establish my covenant with you; Neither shall all flesh be cut off anymore by the waters of a flood; Now this shall there anymore be a flood to destroy the earth. 12. And God said, this is the token of the covenant which I make between me and you and every living creature that is with you, for perpetual generations: 13. I do set my bow in the cloud, and it shall be for a token of a covenant between me and the earth. 14. And it shall come to pass, when I bring a cloud over the earth, that the bow shall be seen in the cloud: 15. And I will remember my covenant, which is between me and you and every living creature of all flesh; and the waters shall no more become a flood to destroy all flesh. 16. And the bow shall be in the cloud; And I will look upon it, that I may remember the everlasting covenant between God and every living creature of all flesh that is upon the earth. 17. And God said unto Noah, this is the token of the covenant, which I have established between me and all flesh that is upon the earth."

The only way to establish a covenant is through the Blood. The word covenant is the Hebrew word *briyth*, and it is defined as in the sense of cutting, a compact, confederacy and league. It is from the root word *barah* that means to render clear, to clarify, examine, and make bright and purged out. That's what the seven eyes do examine to see those who had been rendered and made clear by the Blood to be able to perceive the anointing of the seven Spirits.

When the Lord God says my bow it is the Hebrew word *qesheth* and means the original sense of bending, a bow for shooting, strength, or the iris, arc, arrow, severe, harden, and stiff-necked. It sounds like the LGBTQ is making it hard for themselves.

The word token is the word owth (oath mentioned 7 times in the KJV Bible), and it means in the sense of appearing, a signal, evidence, mark, miracle, to come with consent as permission for
something to happen or agreement to do something. The seven eyes are looking for the applied blood to be able to be in agreement to be in covenant and to do something for us, which is anointing us with the seven Spirits of God.

The first color of the rainbow is the color red. Now let's look at some revelation from Genesis chapter 37 verse 3," Now Israel loved Joseph more than all his children because he was the son of his old age: and he made him a coat of many colours." Now look at Matthews chapter 27 verses 28 and 35. It reads, "28. and they stripped him and put on him a scarlet robe. 35. And they crucified him, and parted his garments, casting lots: that it might be fulfilled which was spoken by the prophet, they parted my garments among them, and upon my vesture did they cast lots." Jesus is the Lamb and he was covered in a scarlet robe which is a red robe which represents the blood.

So, as we go back to Genesis chapter 37 verse 31, "And they took Joseph's coat, and killed a kid of goats, and *dipped the coat in* ;" the word dipped means immersed or plunged. And the word

49

colors is the Hebrew word *pac* which means palm of the hand or the soul of the foot. Think about Jesus' hands and feet that were pierced and He had shed forth blood. in genesis chapter 46 verse 30 it states, "And Israel said unto Joseph, now let me die, since I have seen thy face because thou art yet alive."

Joseph is alive and his coat was dipped in blood the same way that Jesus is alive, and his body was immersed and plunged in blood. This sounds familiar to Revelation chapter 19 verse 13 when it states, "And he was clothed with a vesture *dipped in **blood**: and his name is called The Word of God."

The slain Lamb has seven eyes, seven horns, and the seven Spirits. The bow, rainbow, and the coat of many colors is dipped in blood like the vesture that Jesus wore that was dipped in Blood. So, every oil at the anointing that's poured out and still forth like arrows by the seven angels of the seven Spirits are covered and dipped in the blood. This bow, the rainbow as we know it is dipped in blood. We know that because it is a covenant and the only way to make a covenant is to shed blood.

The rainbow appears in the heavens in all things even the things in the heavens have been reconciled by the blood. Look at Colossians chapter one verse 20, "And, having made peace through the blood of his cross, by him to reconcile all things unto himself; By him, I say, whether they be things in earth, or things in heaven." The word reconciled is the Greek word *apakatallaso* and it means, to fully reconcile, restore friendly relations between, calls to coexist in harmony, and bring back together.

The root word *katallaso* means to make different and change. we must pray for the release of the seven Spirits and the seven colors of his bow and mark us with a red target for the arrows of the anointing oil as we are covered by the Blood and it reconciles, changes, makes us different, and brings us back together again in harmony with the Lord God. This includes estranged families and addictions, and those imprisoned in bondage. We are reminded of our covenant through the bow the covenant of the Blood.

CPSIA information can be obtained
at www.ICGtesting.com
Printed in the USA
LVHW041515210323
742158LV00015B/1825